Spiritual VITAMINS

Daily nutrients for your Spirit

Rev. Kevin V. Montague

Copyright © 2020 Rev. Kevin V. Montague

All rights reserved. No part of this book may be used or reproduced in any manner whatsoever without the express written permission of the author except for the use of brief quotations in a book review.

ISBN: 978-1-7334432-4-1 (Paperback)
ISBN: 978-1-7334432-5-8 (Epub)

First printing, 2020.

JayMedia Publishing
Laurel, MD 20708

www.publishing.jaymediagroup.net

INTRODUCTION

A vitamin is a chemical that is needed for the human body to work correctly. I believe vitamins are effective ways to enhance the areas of our bodies in need of support for optimum physical, mental, and social performance.

In the same manner, spiritual vitamins are needed for adjustments and a daily boost of supernatural energy to press through life's challenges, daily hurdles, and weekly setbacks.

Spiritual Vitamins are a collection of devotions for daily reading taken from KVM Ministries, LLC's weekly JumpStart Encouragement and Prayer Broadcast. The mission of KVM Ministries, LLC is to "Lead With Power and Serve With Care."

I hope that with each spiritual vitamin read and consumed, divine healing will take place in your body and heart. As YOU grow with confidence in God's power through a relationship with His son Jesus Christ, the living word will encourage your spirit and nourish your soul.

My prayer is and my belief is that you will be victorious as you become stronger daily with each intake of God's word through these spiritual vitamins. May God bless each spiritual vitamin dose as you grow in God's grace through the Holy Spirit.

"Then he said to me, "This is what the Lord says to Zerubbabel: It is not by force nor by strength, but by my Spirit, says the Lord of Heaven's Armies." - Zechariah 4:6 (NLT)

All scripture references are from the New Living Translation (NLT) unless stated otherwise.

SPECIAL THANKS

Kelly Turner

DJ Robbo (Robb Fitzgibbons)

Zylah Harper

Monique White

Dexter Montague

Tracy Montague

Betty Hoskins

Pastor Billy T. Staton, Jr.
and the Providence St. John Baptist Family

KVM Ministries, LLC prayer/financial partners

Family and friends

This book is dedicated to my daughters
Morgan Faith and Logan Hope

…. And to honor my parents, Leroy Montague
and the late Margaret H. Montague

TABLE OF CONTENTS

Shhh…Just Listen   1

Forgive   3

Humble Yourself   5

You Weigh Too Much   7

I'm Blown But I'm Still Blessed   9

PSA Regarding Your Prayers   11

What Are You Thinking?   13

A Lifestyle of Thanksgiving   15

Reflecting on the Faithfulness of God   17

Not Just a Child   19

He's Able   21

Show Me Your Scars   23

Unfinished   25

It's Time to Move   27

Dark Places   29

Refuse   31

Castaways   33

Let Go Your Ego   35

The Waiting Room   37

Level Up – A Godly View   39

Costly Obedience   41

A Lifestyle of Prayer   43

Focus   45

Inside Fruit   47

What's in Your Closet?   49

New Life, New Instructions   51

Driven to Win   53

God's Prized Possession   55

When God Says No   57

Even You   59

A Time in the Wilderness   61

I'm Kept   63

NUTRIENT FOR TODAY

Shhh...Just Listen

Scripture: *Read James 1:19 (NLT)*

Dose:

I notice that most children can be talkers. When you explain the right way to do their homework, in the midst of sharing and giving the proper direction to do it the right way, they interrupt you with their chatter to try explaining their side, their point or what they want.

I think it's an epidemic throughout the land. Everyone wants to talk and no one wants to listen.

Even more importantly, it happens between God and us.

For some of us, God is saying "You hear me alright, but are you really listening and doing what I asked"? And while God is speaking, we can't hear Him because we are giving Him our demands instead of keeping quiet and just listening.

It's funny that we want God to listen to us but we don't listen to Him. Whose words are more important?

When you decide to listen to God, your connection with Him will be strengthened, your relationship with Him will grow, and your love for Him will be displayed all because you decided to Shhhh… and listen.

Imagine that when God is speaking, you stop what you're doing, you refrain from asking God anything or complaining and you just listen to Him. God already knows and perhaps He is giving you what you need while you are talking. Shhhhh…

Just Listen! Then obey and do what He says. He is telling you exactly what you need to make it through another day or to overcome your situation.

Prayer:

Dear God, help me to be quick to listen to you and ready to do what you have said. In Jesus' name I pray. Amen

Result of intake:

NUTRIENT FOR TODAY

Forgive

Scripture: *Read Matthew 6:14-15 (NLT)*

Dose:
_____

The other day, I read a post on Facebook from a person asking how to move forward with life after a betrayal. I thought this was an important question because many struggle with moving forward after they've been wronged.

My answer for the person was to FORGIVE! I know this is hard to do for most but this is the way I've found most effective for me.

To forgive is to cease to feel resentment against the offender or to grant relief from a payment.

To move on with life, you must choose to forgive even when you think they don't deserve it or it's uncomfortable to do. Forgiving others releases you from the hurt and damage attached to you so you can go on with your life without a thought of them getting what they deserve.

The problem is that many of us want the person to get what we believe they deserve. But we forget that someone forgave us and we didn't get what we deserved when we did someone wrong.

Scripture says this in Matthew 6:14-15:
If you forgive those who sin against you, your heavenly Father will forgive you. But if you refuse to forgive others, your Father will not forgive your sins.

You say, "I may forgive but not forget." I understand that but forgetting is choosing not to allow the person or the action to affect or control your present and future any longer.

Forgive often and move on with your life. Life is too short to allow anyone or anything to keep you in any form of bondage and from the great things God has waiting for you.

Prayer:
_____

Dear God, help me to forgive the offense and the person so that I can go on with my life in victory. In Jesus' name I pray. Amen.

Result of intake:
_____

NUTRIENT FOR TODAY

Humble Yourself

Scripture: *Read 1 Peter 5:5 (NLT)*

Dose:
_____

Humility is the quality of thinking about the needs of others before your own. Pride is a feeling of deep pleasure or satisfaction derived from one's own achievements. Arrogance is another word for pride. It's thinking more highly of yourself than you ought to and starting to feel you have made it or arrived.

I've often seen how prideful people, instead of humbling themselves, suddenly take a fall. One minute they're on top of the world, the next minute they're trying to figure out what happened.

The problem is that they stopped recognizing who it is that allowed them to achieve and started to think they were in control and made it happen on their own. It's easy to start reading and believing our own headlines but know this... God opposes the proud but gives grace to the humble.

Scripture says this: All of you, dress yourselves in humility and then it says to humble yourselves under the mighty power of God, and at the right time, (here's a promise) He will lift you up in honor.

Just as you put on your clothes to go off to work or school daily, humble yourself daily in submission to God, He promises that when you do, there is a next level He will take you to.

Today, save yourself from the pain of being humbled. Consider working on humbling yourself before God does. Rejoice in knowing that when you properly give God His due respect and honor, He promises to take you higher than you could ever go on your own.

Prayer:

Dear God, help me to humble myself daily and remember that I am who I am because of you and not because of anything I have done. In Jesus' name I pray. Amen.

Result of intake:

SPIRITUAL VITAMINS

NUTRIENT FOR TODAY

You Weigh Too Much

Scripture: *Read Hebrews 12:1-2 (NLT)*

Dose:
_____

Life is full of races. At times, it's an all-out sprint and at other times, it's a marathon.

When you look at runners in a track meet, notice that many aren't wearing anything heavy and their clothes are light. Their shoes are lightweight too. They aren't carrying their gym bag either. They just have what they need to run the fastest time.

The problem is that many of us are carrying things that are slowing us down. Those things are heavy and instead of helping us to run our race to win, it's slowing us down and we are losing the races we were designed to win. What things might that be? People, relationships, wrong attitudes, bad habits, addictions, anger and forgiveness issues are just a few.

How do you strip off things that you don't need? You do so by looking at Jesus Christ who is the image of the perfect runner. Our goal is to look like Him so we should only carry what we see Him carrying. If you have something or someone in your life that you don't see in the image of Christ, then strip it off and out of your life. It's weighing you down. Now, you can run with endurance the fastest race possible.

You must decide to strip off whatever it is that is slowing you down from effectively running the races of your life that God wants you to finish and finish strong.

Prayer:

Dear God, help me identify those things that are weighing me down from being an effective runner for you and help me remove them so I can finish the race in victory. In Jesus' name I pray. Amen.

Result of intake:

NUTRIENT FOR TODAY

I'm Blown But I'm Still Blessed

Scripture: *Read Isaiah 55:8-9 (NLT)*

Dose:

Something happened recently and I was so blown (disappointed). I was disappointed because someone who I had an expectation to accomplish something for me and others didn't come through and dropped the ball. This caused frustration and anger.

Have you ever been blown or disappointed? The problem with that is we allow others to cause a reaction from us that could change our next actions and thoughts. When we give in to disappointment, the effects on what we do can create a barrier between us and others as well as a disconnect with God.

Did you know your disappointments can be what you need to get you closer to your purpose and to God?

Here are 4 things to consider when you are blown:

1. **Pray** - Pray for the person who disappointed you that this will not be a trend in their life but also pray for yourself that you don't react like you want to as well.
2. **Perceive** - Consider that God is using this disappointment (or light affliction) to move you away from something or to move you to Him and your purpose.
3. **Praise** - Praise Him for what He has done and is doing even when you don't understand His ways or thoughts in the matter.

4. Press on - Don't spend precious time dwelling on the person or what happened. You still have a goal and a prize. Get up and press on.

Scripture says in Isaiah 55:8-9 (NLT) – "My thoughts are nothing like your thoughts," says the Lord. "And my ways are far beyond anything you could imagine. For just as the heavens are higher than the earth, so my ways are higher than your ways and my thoughts higher than your thoughts."

I want to encourage you to stop giving people control of your actions and emotions based on what they do or don't do for you. Take back control of YOU! Even though you are blown and disappointed, know that God hasn't left you. He allowed this to happen and it's still part of His plan to bless you. You are blown but you are still blessed.

Prayer:

> Dear God, help us to see what you are doing in our moments of disappointment and we thank you because we know if you allowed it, you also have a greater plan to bless us. In Jesus' name I pray. Amen.

Result of intake:

SPIRITUAL VITAMINS

NUTRIENT FOR TODAY

PSA Regarding Your Prayers

Scripture: *Read Luke 22:42 (NLT)*

Dose:

Do you remember this prayer? "Now I lay me down to sleep, I pray the Lord my soul to keep; if I die before I wake, I pray the Lord my soul to take. Amen"

This is a wonderful prayer for children. Many of us still say prayers we learned when we were a child and our faith walk, relationship and conversation with God is still on a childlike level. To paraphrase a scripture, when I was a child, I spoke like a child and acted like a child. Now, I am grown, I don't say and act like I did when I was a child. This includes how we pray, what we pray for, and who we pray for. Your prayers should not always be about you and your needs.

One of the main reasons your prayers aren't giving you the desired results is there is too much of "YOU" in your prayers. I have a Public Service Announcement (PSA) for you regarding your prayers now that you are grown up. I have learned these 3 things:

P - Be *persistent* in asking God. He can handle it and you aren't bugging him either. Know that as you are asking, God also will show you exactly what you need versus only what you want.

S - Allow God to *sift* you as you pray. To sift means to remove the things that are not useful. God wants to remove the selfish side of you out of the prayer and perhaps have you pray for others. Then, as you submit to the removal, your prayer will be answered and you won't even realize it.

A - *Accept* the will of God above your own. God's will for our lives should supersede what our desire is every time.

Why?

His plan, His answer, His process and His time frame is what's best for our life. Accept it.

Right before Jesus was betrayed by Judas and arrested, He said something major removing His will from the prayer.

Prayer:

Dear God, help us to grow up in our faith and in our prayer life. Mature our relationship with you and remove the selfishness in our communication to you and let us consider the needs of others. In Jesus name I pray. Amen.

Result of intake:

NUTRIENT FOR TODAY

What Are You Thinking?

Scripture: *Read Philippians 4:8-9 (NLT)*

Dose:
_____

Are you a negative thinker? When going through a situation or even a process, do you have thoughts of doom and gloom or woe is me? Do you say to yourself, "I failed this test so I probably will fail the next one" or "Things are bad and they will only get even worse."

I thought like that for a long time and my problem, like many of you, is that I am accustomed to thinking negative, negative, negative. Negative thinking is our mind's first option when it should be positive, positive, and Godly.

Today, I want you to consider changing from being a downward thinker to a look up and above thinker because negative thoughts are trained to destroy you, your purpose, and your future.

I believe that once you replace negative thoughts of self-disappointment, defeat, and destruction with Godly ones, you'll start having Godly or kingdom results.

I want to encourage you to train your mind to see God in everything. I believe kingdom thinking is a choice and the joy of your life depends on the quality of your thoughts.

How do you change your thinking?

What do Godly thoughts look like?

I. Pray to have the mind of God – Lord guard my mind from negative thinking and my heart from negative people. The old folk would say, "God be my mind-regulator."

II. Fix your thinking – adjust your mind and fasten onto Godly thinking based on what God says about you in His word and your purpose.

III. Practice – You must do this daily. Practice will make permanent.

Prayer:

Dear God, condition my mind through what your word says about me to think positive and to be a Godly thinker instead of a negative thinker. Give me the mindset to know through Christ, I can do all things. In Jesus' name I pray. Amen

Result of intake:

NUTRIENT FOR TODAY

A Lifestyle of Thanksgiving

Scripture: *Read 1 Thessalonians 5:18 (NLT)*

Dose:
_____

Thanksgiving is the expression of gratitude especially to God. Expressing gratefulness and being thankful to Him for everything He has done, is doing and will do. What He will do is our hope and it's our future expectation based upon our relationship with Him. I am grateful that His word says He is committed to do for His children and heirs.

But I want to change the definition to not just an expression of gratitude but a lifestyle of expressing gratitude to God or a lifestyle of thanksgiving. A lifestyle is defined as a particular way of living. It is a mode of living.

Here's a question: Did you know that a lifestyle of thanksgiving is expressed by what comes out of your mouth and the way you live? It is your attitude in all conditions, circumstances, and challenges.

The problem for many of us is we are more accustomed to complaining outwardly or grumbling inwardly. When we do this, God isn't pleased. If you are a complainer or a grumbler, go ahead and raise your hand.

So, how can you make thanksgiving a lifestyle when you see no way out of your situation and circumstances and your issues are growing? Choose and start to make thanksgiving a lifestyle by considering not the present but the future. Remember everything that God has promised to you when you live for Him, trust in Him and surrender your life to Him. You may not feel God blessing you in your present but know He is and will continue to do this even more in the future. Look forward. Greater things are coming your way.

Prayer:

Dear God, help me as an heir of Christ with all of the benefits as His child to give you thanks in all circumstances as a lifestyle. Help me God to not look at my present but to look forward to my future which is full of promises, blessings, joy, and sealed in you as I live a lifestyle of thanksgiving. In Jesus' name I pray. Amen.

Result of intake:

NUTRIENT FOR TODAY

Reflecting on the Faithfulness of God

Scripture: *Read Lamentations 3:22-24 (NLT)*

Dose:
_____

Recently, I celebrated my birthday. I'm so grateful to God for all the blessings throughout my many years on earth. As I sat and reflected on my life, quickly the not so good things came to my mind from elementary to college and from childhood to adulthood.

I thought about my failures and mistakes, disappointments, missed opportunities and battles lost. Most of these were because of decisions I made and even blamed others instead of saying I was the reason for these things.

I was so tempted to complain but God reminded me that in spite of these things, He has never left me and has blessed me through everything.

Even when I wasn't faithful to him, He was faithful to me. God is merciful and gracious too.

I want to encourage you that wherever you are in life and whatever you are going through, to reflect back over your life and look at all you made it through and survived all because of God's faithfulness to you, His child.

Let God remind you of everything He has done for you, how you overcame, what you conquered, how you survived, how He kept you from falling and how He made a way out of a no way situation.

As the song says, "He's a way maker, miracle worker, and promise keeper." That's just who God is. So today…Rejoice in the Lord because He loves you more than you can imagine.

The lyrics to a great hymn say, "Great is thy faithfulness, morning by morning, new mercies I see, all I have needed, thy hand has provided, great is thy faithfulness, Lord unto me."

Prayer:

Thank you, God, for your never-ending faithfulness. In Jesus' name, Amen.

Result of intake:

NUTRIENT FOR TODAY

Not Just a Child

Scripture: *Read John 3:16 & Isaiah 9:6-7 (NLT)*

Dose:
_____

During Christmas season, I enjoy watching movies. One of my favorite movies is *Talledegga Nights*. In the movie, the main character, Ricky Bobby said a prayer, "Dear eight-pound, six-ounce, newborn baby Jesus, in your golden fleece diapers, with your curled-up, fat, balled-up little fists pawin' at the air." Ricky Bobby prayed like this because he only connected with the baby version of Jesus and throughout the movie, Ricky and all the other characters only viewed Jesus as a child with no power, no provision, no purpose, no position, and no impact.

I want you to know that Jesus was not just a child. To God, He was much more than a child but a son ... His son and His one and only son.

John 3:16 says, For God so loved the world that He gave not just a child but His begotten son. His son is unique, one of a kind, and in a class all by himself. Jesus is God's special son.

Many people only look at Jesus as a child or baby swaddled in cloth and lying in a manager/feeding trough. Not looking at Him as special, we will miss the blessing of knowing Him as the son of God and Lord and Savior. He is our healer of sickness, our joy in our sadness, our peace in times of trouble, our counselor when we need direction, and much more.

My question to you is: Do you see Him as just any child or as God's son, the Messiah, and the one who came to save you from your sins?

Isaiah 9:6-7 says, "For a child is born to us, a son is given to us. The government will rest on His shoulders. And He will be called: Wonderful Counselor, Mighty God, Everlasting Father, Prince of Peace. His government and its peace will never end."

Prayer:

Dear God, help me to change my view about the Christmas season and your son and give you thanks for giving me the greatest gift of them all through your son Jesus the Christ. In Jesus' name I pray. Amen

Result of intake:

NUTRIENT FOR TODAY

He's Able

Scripture: *Read Ephesians 3:20 (NLT)*

Dose:

Sometimes life can be so difficult that you wonder what is God doing. You ask yourself questions like: Does God hear me? Does God see what I am going through? Does God see my tears? Where are you God? I know I have on many occasions.

When God doesn't answer me the way I want or when I want Him to, then I become negative saying, "I doubt that God will save me from my troubles. I don't believe God will deliver me from this situation. God isn't strong enough to heal me from pains.

I want you to know that yes God is able. I am a living witness that He really is able.

We will tell people He is able but really we don't believe it. The phrase He is able is a cliché or lyrics to a song. In our speech and actions, our confidence in God's ability to come through for us is low or often times doesn't exist. God sees, knows, and has a plan for everything that you are going through even though you may not understand.

As you develop your relationship with God, your level of trust in Him will grow.

Proverbs 3:5 says, "Trust in the Lord with all your heart; do not depend on your own understanding."

When you abandon your level of education and understanding, then you will be able to say the following:

"Now all glory to God, who is able, through His mighty power at work within us, to accomplish infinitely more than we might ask or think." - Ephesians 3:20

Prayer:

Dear God, help me to remember all the times I felt you were not able and yet you never left me and came through for me. Help my doubt and unbelief to trust in you to be more than able in my life. In Jesus' name I pray. Amen.

Result of intake:

NUTRIENT FOR TODAY

Show Me Your Scars

Scripture: *Read Revelations 12:11 (NLT)*

Dose: _____

All of us have been wounded. As a result, we have scars. I remember growing up I had a skateboard accident that left me battered and bruised. My ego and emotions were battered and bruised too. However, the wounds (physical, emotional, and psychological) healed and produced scars.

Some scars (external and internal) are visible where you see the marking and others are deep and hidden but there is scar tissue. When the accident or affliction happened, it formed a wound. But I am glad wounds do heal although they leave you a scar as a reminder.

What have you overcome that others need to know so that they can overcome too? The problem is we are ashamed to share our scars because it is still painful to talk about what we have been through. The key word is **"through"**. You overcame because you heard the testimony about how someone was wounded, they received the scar and yet, they survived it.

There are 3 things scars will do when you trust God and share your story of how you received them. They remind you of:
1. What you have been through and survived
2. What the enemy tried but failed
3. What others can go through and overcome too

Scripture reads:
"And they have defeated him by the blood of the Lamb and by their testimony. " – Revelation 12:11

Prayer:

Dear God, give me the confidence in your son to give me boldness to share my past to help someone overcome their issues and problems. In Jesus' name I pray. Amen

Result of intake:

SPIRITUAL VITAMINS

NUTRIENT FOR TODAY

Unfinished

Scripture: *Read Exodus 3:14-17 (NLT)*

Dose:

When the year is almost over, I get excited. I look back throughout the year and recall many of the things I have accomplished. However, I conveniently moved around all of the things I didn't get accomplished. If you looked back over the course of the year, you probably would too. You know the thing or things that you started, and you had everything you needed to finish it, but for some reason, you still haven't completed it. UNFINISHED. For some, it's another year and no progress.

- Applying for a job
- Opening a business
- Going back to school and to church
- Forgiving a loved one

Are any of these things unfinished in your life?

In the Bible, God told the people of Israel to go and possess the land flowing with milk and honey even though there were giants already in the land. However, it took them a long time to finish this assignment because like many of us, there were 4 reasons they struggled to finish:

Fear - I am not strong enough or smart enough and I don't have enough resources at my disposal.

Assumptions - I know I can't because someone told me I couldn't.

Complacency - I am good where I am right here. I don't need to do anything else.

Trust-less - I am trusting my instincts versus trusting God.

The problem is that even though the children of Israel sent a group to bring back evidence (huge grapes in their hands) that the land was there, and they could possess it, they came up with these reasons to leave the task UNFINISHED.

By faith, I no longer walk in fear, listen to other's assumptions, or find myself at a standstill and unable to trust God. Now, I listen to God's voice and complete what is unfinished in my life.

Prayer:

Dear God, let me not rest until I finish what you assigned to me. In Jesus' name I pray. Amen

Result of intake:

SPIRITUAL VITAMINS

NUTRIENT FOR TODAY

It's Time to Move

Scripture: *Read Genesis 19 (NLT)*

Dose:
_____

I've been watching a lot of HGTV and one of my favorite shows is *Love It or List It*. The show's purpose is to have you make a decision to fix up your house or move to a better house.

The old house normally needs a lot of work. Plumbing issues, roof damage, or other major problems are encountered that would have the family consider listing. Costly repairs usually are needed if they want their old home to be their dream home. But one host, an interior designer, asks the couple if doing the repair is worth the cost.

The other host, a realtor, goes and discovers a great house that meets all of their needs and gives them a better future.

In Genesis 19, Lot and his family were approached by an angel (a messenger) and told to flee from their old location (Sodom and Gomorrah - an ungodly place of living) which God was preparing to destroy and go quickly to a place of prosperity flowing with milk and honey... a life of purpose called Canaan.

On today, I come to you as a messenger to say it's time to move from your old mindset (of doubt, defeat, disappointment, fear, failure, and anger) and go quickly into a new mindset, leaving all those things behind you and walking into a new vision, new mission in life, and new opportunities. You can't hesitate like Lot and you can't look back like Lot's wife. Lot's wife suffered the consequence of looking back on her life and ended up a pillar of salt. If we asked Lot's wife a question of was it worth it, she probably would say no. Let me ask you, is it worth staying in your past versus moving into your future fully? Please don't be like Lot's wife and never obtain God's best for your life.

I want to encourage you that even though you may be afraid, it's time to move and leave your troubles behind you and walk forward with the mindset of this is your year to flow, to conqueror, to overcome, and to receive everything that God has already prepared for you. It's time to move!

Prayer:

Dear God, give me the faith to trust you and move into the present year and not look back into my past and the things that would keep me from striving and thriving. Thank you for speaking to me and telling me it's time to move, and in obedience, I will now move. In Jesus' name I pray. Amen

Result of intake:

NUTRIENT FOR TODAY

Dark Places

Scripture: *Read John 3:21 (NLT)*

Dose:
_____

Have you ever been in a dark place? I am not talking about a physical place absent from light but in a situation or position where you are unable to see your next steps of how to get out of it or things aren't going well and in spite of all you have tried to do on your own, you just are not progressing or moving ahead.

Dark places are part of life. But the dark places aren't meant for you to stay there. In your dark places, you learn to be a better you and to seek the light - God. However, some get comfortable in the dark places and they stay there and never come out.

Scripture says this: But those who do what is right **come to the light** so others can see that they are doing what God wants.

I want to encourage you to do the right thing and come out of your dark places so that you live a life of joy, peace and abundance …and so that others can see they can come out too.

Know that God is very present and a help in times of trouble and darkness. He is still God even in your darkest places and moments. God and the word of God is a lamp to guide your feet and a light to your path.

I want to encourage you by saying there is a light in your dark place. Darkness always gives way to the light.

Prayer:

Dear God, shine your light even brighter in my dark moments so I can find my way out of the darkness and find you. In Jesus' name I pray. Amen

Result of intake:

NUTRIENT FOR TODAY

Refuse

Scripture: *Read James 4:7 (NLT)*

Dose:

Remember when you were a child and you were given veggies and you refused to eat them? Imagine if you had the same stubbornness and REFUSED in other ways such as your relationships and your finances.

By definition, to REFUSE is to indicate or show that one is not willing to do something, or not willing to accept or grant something offered or requested...to stand your ground, or resist your enemy.

James 4:7 says:

"So humble yourselves before God. Resist (REFUSE) the devil, and he will flee from you."

In other words, follow God and His word and allow Him to guide you and REFUSE anything or anyone that is taking your energy and your time instead of pushing you to your purpose.

One of the most memorable lines from the Lord of the Rings movies is when Gandalf, with a sword in one hand and a staff in the other, stands up, stands firm, and stands with confidence before the monster and enemy, saying "You shall not pass."

David said something similar to the giant Goliath and refused to let him run all over him and his people.

Today, is your time to use the powerful word that God has given you to REFUSE the advancement or the control of others.

It's the word NO. I am giving you permission to use the words NO and REFUSE.

REFUSE and take back control.... **REFUSE** and get your mind right... **REFUSE** and get your thoughts right... **REFUSE** and get your health back... **REFUSE** and get your finances back in order... **REFUSE** and get your family or your children or your spouse back... **REFUSE** and get your life back... your whole life back.

Prayer:

> Dear God, help me to remain in control of my life and to stand strong and confident when I REFUSE anyone or anything that rises up or stands in my way of achieving my purpose and living my best life in you. In Jesus' name I pray. Amen

Result of intake:

SPIRITUAL VITAMINS

NUTRIENT FOR TODAY

Castaways

Scripture: *Read 1 Peter 5:6-7 (NLT)*

Dose: _____

Remember the show Gilligan's Island? It was about seven men and women stranded on an uncharted island following a torrential storm. They were considered castaways.

A castaway by definition is an adjective describing a person who was thrown away or rejected.

We all are castaways or have been rejected or thrown away for many reasons including who we place our trust in. We were rejected by our friends, families, spouses, communities, and our jobs. You may feel you are no longer needed and have been tossed aside. Yes… you are castaways but God accepts you as you are and on today, I am giving the word a new definition and I believe God wants all of us to be His castaways.

The Bible says this in 1 Peter 5:6-7 (NKJV)
"Therefore humble yourselves under the mighty hand of God, that He may exalt you in due time, casting all your care upon Him, for He cares for you."

To be His castaway, you must surrender your thoughts of handling issues and problems on your own to God. Give God everything: your personal worries, secret problems, and past pains.

I want to encourage you to be God's castaway and cast all your cares upon Him, for He cares for you. God can handle whatever you are going through but you must decide to cast it to Him. I believe you have been carrying the pain, the feelings and emotions too long. When you give your cares to God, He is going to give you what you need to restore you, support you, strengthen you and plant you on the solid rock which is Jesus Christ.

Prayer:

Dear God, help me to see I can't handle my problems on my own and trust in you knowing that you certainly can. In Jesus' name I pray. Amen

Result of intake:

SPIRITUAL VITAMINS

NUTRIENT FOR TODAY

Let Go Your Ego

Scripture: *Read Proverbs 3:6 (NLT)*

Dose:

There was a Kellogg's commercial where the dad and his son were at their breakfast table and the toaster popped up an Eggo waffle. They both grab it and they won't budge to give it up and they say "L'eggo My EGGO!" I want to change it to say **Let Go Your Ego!**

Often, it's our ego that is keeping us from receiving what God has for us. Our ego takes the credit for the things we didn't earn, and we didn't have the ability to accomplish on our own.

It was neither your wealth, education, status nor athleticism that got you what you have or where you are. **Let Go Your Ego.**

When you take credit for what God has done or is doing in your life, God gets jealous and stops guiding you to your purpose. **Let Go Your Ego.**

Proverbs 3:6 says, in all your ways acknowledge Him and He will direct your paths.

Notice it doesn't say in some of your ways, or when it's convenient, or when it feels good or some of the time.

If you want to have clear direction in your life, humble yourself in everything you say and do and **Let Go Your Ego.** God cannot and will not show you the way to go if your ego is blocking Him from getting to your heart.

On today, I want to encourage you to not be credit takers (taking His credit) and stop grabbing His glory for your own! It's not yours to take. It's too big for you to handle and take credit for.

He earned the right to be glorified. You didn't. Being crucified, dying on the cross and getting up out of the grave earned Him the right to be glorified. So, **Let Go Your Ego** and watch how God moves you from one level to the next.

Prayer:

Dear God, forgive me for allowing my pride to rise up and my ego to get in the way of you directing my paths to my purpose. Today, I give you the honor and glory for who I am, all that I have and ever will be. I give you thanks for the things you have done. In Jesus' name I pray. Amen

Result of intake:

NUTRIENT FOR TODAY

The Waiting Room

Scripture: *Read Philippians 4:6-7 (NLT)*

Dose:
_____

Recently, I spent hours in a hospital waiting room. I am sure many of you have as well. Before going in to see the doctor, hospitals have you waiting with others who either have a need to see the doctor or are waiting for someone else to be seen. While I was there, I noticed some who were very active. They were reading a book or newspaper, on their phone talking or texting someone or playing a game, eating or watching TV. Others were just sitting there and perhaps worrying about what was going on with them or how they will pay the bills and others were just sleeping.

The problem with this is that it's a great time to be productive and get things accomplished.

Like in a hospital waiting room, most of us are in a spiritual waiting room, waiting on God to come through for us. We may be in a holding pattern waiting for God to answer prayers for healing, a job, to put back together a relationship, or just to mend a broken heart.

I want to encourage you to be active in your faith while you wait. Be productive because you still have things to do to be a better you.

So, what should you do while you are waiting on God to see you through?

The Bible says this Philippians 4:6-7 (NKJV):

"Be anxious for nothing, but in everything by prayer and supplication, with thanksgiving, let your requests be made known to God; and the peace of God, which surpasses all understanding, will guard your hearts and minds through Christ Jesus."

Notice it doesn't say just sit there but to be active not worrying, but praying about everything and thanking God for supplying your needs. Thank Him for what He's going to do and ask Him for everything you stand in the need of. Then, He says I am going to give you peace that is going to blow your mind while guarding your heart and mind through your faith in His son Jesus.

It's active faith that makes your waiting more bearable because God is with you and giving you what you need until He comes through. Be encouraged and active in your Waiting Room.

Prayer:

Thank you, God, for your waiting room. Your waiting room allows me to actively seek you and draw closer to you. I am grateful you haven't left me there alone, but you are preparing to bring me to where my needs and desires will be met. I rejoice and give you praise. In Jesus' name I pray. Amen

Result of intake:

SPIRITUAL VITAMINS

NUTRIENT FOR TODAY

Level Up – A Godly View

Scripture: *Read Colossians 3:1-2 (NLT)*

Dose:

When looking at half a glass of water, we have one of these views: The glass is half empty or half full.

Often times in our problems and situations, our viewpoint is one that isn't seeing all that is going on and will cause us to be disappointed, in despair, dismayed and feeling defeated. But what if we change our heart and mind and say, "I praise God for allowing me to have just enough water to fill me and quench my thirst right now."

I want to encourage you to raise your thoughts and understanding beyond what you currently see, change the way you are viewing your life, and Level Up by looking at it from a Godly view. The level that God wants you to see your issue or situation from is one that will give you peace and hope knowing that God is in control and He is already working it out for your good.

The Bible says this in Colossians 3:1-2 (NIV):

"Since, then, you have been raised with Christ, set your hearts on things above, where Christ is, seated at the right hand of God. Set your minds on things above, not on earthly things."

To set means to intentionally look at the problem, pain, and present situation from God's eyes. This means I am going to Level Up by changing my heart and my mind and not thinking doom and gloom (and my life will never change). Instead,

I am going to Level Up because I am now seeing my circumstances are different and it is going to get better if I can hold on a little while longer.

So…. Level up in your finances, marriage, health, business or job and with your children.

Level up and believe I will overcome; I will conquer and I will be victorious because there is victory in Jesus Christ.

Prayer:

> Dear God, help me to Level Up in my heart and mind to see my life from your view point. Then, I will find peace and hope knowing your plan is working for my good. In Jesus' name I pray. Amen

Result of intake:

NUTRIENT FOR TODAY

Costly Obedience

Scripture: *Read Matthew 5:43-45 (NLT)*

Dose:
_____

Pastor Steve Furtick said, "When you ask God to do the impossible, He usually instructs you to do something uncomfortable and inconvenient."

In other words, that "something" will reveal to God whether you will fully obey or continue to be in control of your life pushing Him further away.

Obeying God can be difficult because it will cause you to give up your past thoughts, mindset, and attitude.

When you have an enemy or a hater, the natural reaction is to confront them, give them a piece of your mind and to attack. You want to tell them where they can go and how fast they should get there.

But the Bible says:

"You have heard the law that says, 'Love your neighbor' and hate your enemy. But I say, love your enemies! Pray for those who persecute you! In that way, you will be acting as true children of your Father in heaven." - Matthew 5:43-45

"Do not seek revenge or bear a grudge against a fellow Israelite, but love your neighbor as yourself. I am the Lord"- Leviticus 19:18

Hold up, are you saying to be considered a child of God, you have to love and pray for your haters? Yes! In order to obey God, you must follow His directions. This means, it's going to cost you the way you normally would react. Your attitude will need to change to line up with God's attitude and your heart and actions now must obey Him by loving people who have hated on you and you may not even like.

To obey God is going to be difficult and uncomfortable and will cost you giving up the old way of acting and the "prideful, arrogant, and strong you" that normally is in control keeping you from obtaining the blessings God has stored up for you.

It was once said: "Obedience may be costly but the end result is priceless". So, the blessing of God is waiting for you to simply obey Him even if it costs you, You!

Prayer:

Dear God, help me to give up my old mindset, my thoughts of revenge, and my attitude in order to follow and obey you. Give me strength to do this and bless me for my obedience to you in Jesus' name I pray, Amen.

Result of intake:

NUTRIENT FOR TODAY

A Lifestyle of Prayer

Scripture: *Read James 5:16-18 (NLT)*

Dose:
_____

People ask me all of the time, why do I pray? I tell them because my relationship with God is so important to me. Prayer connects me with God's power, strength, information, and direction. It also gives me an opportunity to thank Him, to praise Him, to worship Him and to confess when I am wrong and ask for forgiveness. It gives me an opportunity to be humble and pray for other people and not solely about myself. All of this helps me develop a real relationship with Him.

Usually, there is a follow-up question, how often do I pray? I tell them I pray all of the time. First Thessalonians 5:17 (NKJV), says, "Pray without ceasing…" The Greek word for "without ceasing" is adialeiptos, which doesn't mean nonstop — but actually means constantly recurring.

I am constantly praying because praying has now become a lifestyle and is also a priority. I have made my time with God a priority.

But for some people, they pray occasionally and that is only when they are sick, need bills to be paid, or are in trouble. Prayer should never be an exit plan.

I am grateful that through constant prayer in the good times and the bad times, I receive the strength, encouragement and instructions that will help me make the right choices and decisions to keep me from trouble that I tend to put myself in.

When prayer is a lifestyle, miracles and other amazing things happen.

Like prophet Elijah, when you prioritize prayer as a lifestyle, it will produce wonderful results including miracles. Let's make prayer a lifestyle today.

Prayer:

Dear God, thank you for the opportunity to pray to you. Impress upon my heart the need for a deeper and consistent relationship with you so that prayer isn't a chore but a lifestyle. In Jesus' name I pray. Amen.

Result of intake:

SPIRITUAL VITAMINS

NUTRIENT FOR TODAY

Focus

Scripture: *Read Philippians 3:13-14 (NLT)*

Dose:
_____

Life is a race and everyone has a goal or target that they are trying to reach whether it is a financial goal and to make more money, get a better job with benefits, obtain a renewed relationship with a friend or to help their children get to college. Everyone has a personal goal or target.

What is your goal today?

To reach the goal, you must **FOCUS**. To **FOCUS** means to look intently and work towards something, regardless of external factors, to the end. You **FOCUS** on what it takes to get there, ask questions, read, meet with people, and of course seek God and pray.

However, whenever you have to **FOCUS**, it is so easy to become distracted. Distractions come from past disappointments, present overwhelming difficulties, the pain of a relationship, negative people, or simply people guiding you away from the path to your goal.

But today, I want to encourage you to remain focused on the way to your goal and your prize. Don't allow those things or even people to veer you off course. Do whatever it takes to get rid of those things that are setting you up for failure instead of setting you up to win.

Hebrews 12:1-2

Therefore, since we are surrounded by such a huge crowd of witnesses to the life of faith, let us strip off every weight that slows us down, especially the sin that so easily trips us up. And let us run with endurance the race God has set before us. We do this by keeping our eyes on Jesus, the champion who initiates and perfects our faith.

When your **FOCUS** is on Christ, He will guide you along the path and make it easy to remove whatever it is that is blurring your vision or slowing you down from running and enduring your race to win.

At the end, Christ won the race and now we call Him champion. We can win too.

So, what's your goal today? That's great. Now… **FOCUS** and remain focused.

Here's an acronym for you for **FOCUS: F**ixed - **O**n - **C**hrist, not ourselves - **U**ntil - **S**uccessful

Prayer:

Dear God, show me those things and people that are blurring my vision or are slowing me down and then give me the wisdom and strength to let those things go so I can win my race and reach my goal in you. In Jesus' name I pray. Amen

Result of intake:

SPIRITUAL VITAMINS

NUTRIENT FOR TODAY

Inside Fruit

Scripture: *Read Galatians 5:22-23 (NLT)*

Dose:
_____

The fruit that the Holy Spirit has produced inside of you is designed to make you similar to Him in every area of your life. God's desire is that we think, act, and live like Christ. To be like Christ, you must understand that the following is packaged up inside of you as a believer. I am talking about joy, peace, patience, kindness, goodness, faithfulness, gentleness, and self-control.

The problem is that these characteristics of Christ are not used much in our lives and they are buried under sorrow, conflict, disobedience, and evil. It's like weeds and rocks in our hearts covering good fruit.

But God has produced the goodness of Christ inside of us. It is up to us to remove the weeds and rocks and allow the fruit to take control of us in our speech, conversation, actions and especially our attitude. We have an abundance of inside fruit to become who God wants us to be which is like His son.

You are thinking that you don't have the ability to be like Christ especially if you have been offended or your day is going bad. But I am here to tell you that you have everything you need inside of you.

You have inside fruit (which is the fruit of the Spirit) and you aren't restricted in how the fruit is given to others. I want to encourage you that when you are in a difficult situation or life isn't going well, remember to be like Christ according to His Word and allow the fruit that has been produced inside you to give the proper Christlike response.

Blessings and favor will be given to you as a result of you submitting and surrendering to His will and not yours.

Prayer:

Dear God, thank you God for your son who loved me enough to leave the Holy Spirit to help me when I am in need and to produce in me the ability to live an amazing life and to be like you. Help me God to remove anything that would block my fruit and my desire to be Christlike. In Jesus' name I pray. Amen

Result of intake:

SPIRITUAL VITAMINS

NUTRIENT FOR TODAY

What's in Your Closet?

Scripture: *Read Colossians 3:12-15 (NLT)*

Dose:

Each morning, I check my weather app to see what the weather will be. One of the first things I do is go into my closet and figure out what I want to put on. I have the shirts on one side, shoes on another side, my sweatshirts here and my suits are elsewhere. There are different articles of clothing for a different look, opportunity and occasion. Fun, casual, business, and formal looks for different encounters and opportunities.

The bible says to put clothes on to look like Christ or to reflect who Christ is in our life and our hearts.

However, those clothes aren't the first things we put on (or are in our hearts) when we leave the house and encounter conflict and people who push our buttons. We have in our hearts and minds things that reflect our old nature of dealing with issues and problems instead of following the word of God and clothing ourselves to look, act, and speak in a way that will represent the Christ we serve.

Since we have a new nature in Christ, I encourage you to put on the right clothes daily to represent Christ and watch how those who come against you will ask you questions to give you the opportunity to share a little deeper about what is in your closet and the clothes you put on today.

Prayer:

Dear God, help me to put on the right clothes so I can look like you to a world who rarely sees you. Show me what needs to be removed from my heart and what needs to be placed inside so that when people see me, they see your son Jesus the Christ. In Jesus' name I pray. Amen

Result of intake:

SPIRITUAL VITAMINS

NUTRIENT FOR TODAY

New Life, New Instructions

Scripture: *Read 2 Corinthians 5:17 & 1 Timothy 6:11-14 (NLT)*

Dose:
_____

Several months ago, I got rid of my old TV because it wasn't working properly anymore. Even though it was heavy and bulky, I was familiar with how to operate it. So, I purchased a new TV with all the bells and whistles. It took a minute to start using this new TV properly because I was so familiar with the old one. The instructions were different. The remote was different. Even the way I viewed shows was different. When I began to rely on the new instructions, I was able to enjoy the new TV.

I just want to remind you as a believer in Jesus Christ, you are a new person and have a new life. This means that the old way to go about living your life won't work with how you are now as a new person in Christ. The old instructions that you are familiar with can no longer be used to live a new life in Christ.

2 Corinthians 5:17 says:

This means that anyone who belongs to Christ has become a new person. The old life is gone; a new life has begun!

The problem is that many people struggle living a Christian life because they pick up the old instructions of living and try to apply it to the new person God has called you to be. The old instructions only work with the old person. You are a new person now in Christ and the old person no longer exist.

Scripture says in 1 Timothy 6:11-12

But you, Timothy, are a man of God; so, run from all these evil things (old instructions). Pursue (new instructions) righteousness and a godly life, along with faith, love, perseverance, and gentleness. Fight the good fight for the true faith. Hold tightly to the eternal life to which God has called you, which you have declared so well before many witnesses.

Remember because you are a new person in Christ, you live under a new set of requirements, responsibilities, or instructions so that your testimony will be considered a good one, one without being questioned.

Prayer:

Dear God, thank you for my new life and new set of instructions that will guide and direct my life. Help me to resist looking at the old manual that I created and to pursue living the life you want for me using the instructions from your word. I ask these things in Jesus' name, Amen.

Result of intake:

NUTRIENT FOR TODAY

Driven to Win

Scripture: *Proverbs 24:30-34*

Dose:

At some point, did you have a dream or project you started to make come true but lost your passion or energy to see it through?

As a matter of fact, if you were to tell the truth, the reason why you haven't finished is because you have gotten lazy.

To be lazy means to be disinclined to activity, not energetic or vigorous, to be slothful and to be a bum.

A person is being lazy if they are able to carry out some activity that they ought to carry out, but are slothful to do so because of the effort involved.

That's a major problem with finishing anything. The Bible says this in Proverbs 24:30-34, "I walked by the field of a lazy person, the vineyard of one with no common sense. I saw that it was overgrown with nettles. It was covered with weeds, and its walls were broken down. Then, as I looked and thought about it, I learned this lesson: A little extra sleep, a little more slumber, a little folding of the hands to rest— then poverty will pounce on you like a bandit; scarcity will attack you like an armed robber."

This proverb is saying the longer you remain lazy, the harder it will be to begin again and the more likely you will lose out on the thing that was meant to prosper you.

Other reasons people lose their drive to win is because they lose focus and the past has a hold on them and they cannot see beyond their present situation/circumstance.

I want to encourage you to be Driven to Win. You start first by readjusting your focus back on your target and like Philippians 3:13-14 says: Forgetting the past and looking forward to what lies ahead, I press on to reach the end of the race and receive the heavenly prize for which God, through Christ Jesus, is calling us.

There is a great prize at the end but you must remain driven to win to the end.

Prayer:

Dear God, thank you for giving me a vision and instructions. Help me keep my drive to win so that I can fulfill my purpose and destiny in you. In Jesus' name I pray. Amen.

Result of intake:

NUTRIENT FOR TODAY

God's Prized Possession

Scripture: *Read James 1:18 (NLT)*

Dose:

I think that it is good to hear that you are important to a business, a team, a corporation, or even a relationship. Your worth, importance, value, and what you bring to the table is needed and appreciated.

My speech and my confidence can be hampered because what I felt I brought to the table wasn't as important as what others have to offer.

Many go through life feeling like they are just not enough and they aren't up to the world standard and they don't bring anything to a business or even to a relationship. You feel like you don't fit and you are alone on an island or a castaway. This leaves you vulnerable to depression and to an enemy who can steal, kill and destroy.

But now that I am in Christ, God has changed all of that. Through His word, He tells me constantly that He loves me and cares about me. There is never a day that goes by that I am not told He loves me and that I am important. I am affirmed of who I am and why I was created. Regardless of when I have a bad day, He has reminders to let me know He is with me and that I am not alone. He tells me that I am His prized possession.

When you are someone's prized possession, you are the most precious thing to them. You are loved and cared for, spoken well of, displayed to others, kept safe and secure from harm, showed off, and talked about. To God, you are His prized possession.

Here are 3 reasons to praise God as His prized possession:

- You are Chosen and given His word
- You were Carefully made
- You are Cherished

So, live life in confidence (not arrogance), hold your head up high at school and at work, walk in the room with boldness and authority, let your swag swing in front of the haters and doubters because you are God's prized possession.

Prayer:

Dear God, thank you for carefully creating me to be special and with love. As a result, I reflect who you are to a world that needs to see they are different and yet loved by you. Thank you, God, for making me in your image with love. In Jesus' name I pray. Amen

Result of intake:

SPIRITUAL VITAMINS

NUTRIENT FOR TODAY

When God Says No

Scripture: *Read Luke 22:42 (NLT)*

Dose:

Jesus went to the Mount of Olives to pray because He would soon be crucified. In Luke 22:42 Jesus said, "if you are willing, please take this cup of suffering (God's plan) away from me. Yet I want your will to be done, not mine."

Recently, I lost someone that was dear to me. Every day, my prayer remained to help me deal with seeing my loved one in this state but also to keep them alive. But on this day, God said, "No."

How could God say no on this day? Could it have been some other day? Could it have been a month from now?

When God says no, is it to punish you?

When God says no, is it to get you back?

When God says no, is it because He doesn't love you? He really does.

When God says no, it is because:

I. God is sovereign and in control.

He's all powerful, holy, and just. He is the creator and ruler of the universe; He is King of Kings and Lord of Lords. He can do whatever He wants to do. He's loving, caring and saving.

He works out everything in conformity with the purpose of His will.

God is in control. It would help if we are mindful of this. It's also saying He loves us and has our best interest in mind. He's in control and we are not. God's plan doesn't say to make sure you are happy, smiling, or comfortable.

II. God has a plan beyond ours.

Jeremiah 29:11

"For I know the plans I have for you," says the Lord. "They are plans for good and not for disaster, to give you a future and a hope."

Save yourself the time and allow God's plan to go forth in your life and stop trying to figure out things on your own. If you want to figure out God, know God's word.

III. God's word can be trusted.

Numbers 23:19 (ESV)

The scripture says, "God is not a man that He should lie, or a son of man that He should change His mind." God can be trusted to do what He has said concerning your life. God's words are pure. They contain nothing worthless or useless. His word is flawless.

God's "no" was carefully thought out so that you can trust in Him more and to build your faith in Him to see you through even the most difficult of times.

Prayer:

Dear God, help me to accept when you say no. I realize it isn't to harm me, but you still care about me and have something greater for me. In Jesus' name I pray, Amen.

Result of intake:

SPIRITUAL VITAMINS

NUTRIENT FOR TODAY

Even You

Scripture: *Read Genesis 32 (NLT)*

Dose:

Throughout the course of history, God has woven certain people into His plan who not by accident or coincidence, have made a mistake or two that resulted in some larger-than-life outcomes. The Bible is filled with stories of people, just like you and me, that have struggled, stumbled, failed and simply just messed up. It's in these "oh, my bad" moments that the Lord teaches us His greatest lessons and He reveals His will along the way. It's also an opportunity to see the power of God's great mercy, grace, and forgiveness.

In the book of Genesis, Jacob was considered shifty and untrustworthy because he stole his brother Esau's birth right. Jacob is a symbol of a past with regret, shame, and failure.

However, in Genesis 32, when running away from his brother and knowing he was wrong, Jacob had an encounter with God and wrestled with God all night to help him be saved from his brother's wrath.

In this all-night wrestling match, we find out this about God:

- **God is not deterred by you** - He isn't pushed away by what you have done (your great transgressions).
- **God is "long suffering" towards you** - He will wait for you to give in to Him and to get some 'act right' in you.

- **God doesn't forsake you** - He doesn't turn his back to you and quit loving you.
- **God is not ashamed of you** - He doesn't cast you aside.

At the end of the match in Genesis 32, God changed Jacob's name to Israel in order to give him purpose. But throughout the bible starting in Exodus, God wanted to remind everyone that He was the God of Isaac, Abraham and Jacob. Yeah… even shady Jacob too.

Regardless of what you have done in your life, the mistakes you have made, and the people you have hurt, God is still the God of "EVEN YOU". He wants you to know that you don't have to look any further for forgiveness and mercy. He is waiting for you to ask Him so He can forgive you and cleanse you from all of the things you have done wrong.

Prayer:

Thank you God for loving EVEN me when I have messed up and done the wrong things. I am so glad you did not cast me aside but made a way for me to come back to you through your son Jesus Christ. I thank you. In Jesus' name I pray. Amen

Result of intake:

SPIRITUAL VITAMINS

NUTRIENT FOR TODAY

A Time in the Wilderness

Scripture: *Read Psalm 63:1-4, 5-9 (NLT)*

Dose: _____

Have you ever felt like you were alone and in a place where no one understands what you are going through? You get up each day and life is still the same and nothing has changed. No new testimonies, no breakthroughs, no miracles. It is an uncomfortable place where you feel distant from others. You are uncertain about what's next in your life. It can be a place of loneliness and discouragement at times especially when you see others appearing to get yours and you just feel like you are existing. You ask God, when will my change come?

If so, you may be having a wilderness experience. A "wilderness experience" is usually thought of as a tough time in which a believer endures discomfort and trials. The things of life are not enjoyable at all, and you feel a lack of encouragement. A "wilderness experience" is often a time of intensified temptation and spiritual attack. It can involve a spiritual, financial, or emotional drought. Having a "wilderness experience" is not necessarily a sign that you sinned; rather, it is a time of God-ordained testing.

In Psalm 63, David has a time in the wilderness of Judah. It was a time of praise and worship, meditation, insight and rejoicing. It isn't a time of doom and gloom, or moping, worrying, or complaining or having a pity party but a useful moment with Him who is a very present help in all times. Can I give you a different perspective of A Time In The Wilderness? Consider this:

Verse 1 - A Time of Intimacy with God - God is closer to you than ever.

Verse 2 - A Time of Remembrance with God - A time when I look back over my life and I think about all He has done.

Verses 3-4 - A Time of Adoration with God - A time where I can exalt and lift up His name because He is good.

Verses 5-8 - A Time of Communion and Thanksgiving with God - It's a time when you can give thanks for the Lord is good, His mercy endures forever.

Verse 9 - A Time of Godly Vision - A time that God shows you further into your purpose and you can rejoice for God is about to do a new thing in your life.

Praise God when you are experiencing a time in the wilderness.

Prayer:

Dear God, even though the time in the wilderness feels uncomfortable, I know it's for my good and You are with me. I can rejoice and give You thanks right now because in a little while I will be out of it. I thank you in advance. In Jesus' name I pray. Amen

Result of intake:

SPIRITUAL VITAMINS

NUTRIENT FOR TODAY

I'm Kept

Scripture: *Read Psalm 121:7-8 (NLT)*

Dose:

Often times, when someone says they are a kept man or a kept woman, it is negative and the person is doing something as a result of what was done for them like an exchange of favors.

But I want to change this up a little bit and look at things from a biblical standpoint of what it means to be "kept."

It means we are reserved, set apart, taken…spoken for, saved, and held. When we're kept by Him, we're provided for by His everlasting love. In fact, we're the apple of His eye and He's always watching out for us. I don't mind being kept by God because there is salvation, safety, protection, and care when God is keeping us.

No matter what we've done, where we've been or how badly our hearts are shattered, God remains faithful to us. Whether we've been hurt or broken or are responsible for the pain in a relationship, God can still lift us up and keep us. He is the ultimate and eternal promise keeper and won't let us go. God is reliable, stable, watchful, a protector, a deliverer, and will take good care of us forever.

Psalm 121:7-8 (NIV)
The Lord will keep you from all harm—
 He will watch over your life;

> the Lord will watch over your coming and going
> both now and forevermore.

I celebrate being kept by God and I'm good with that. Won't you be as well?

Prayer:

Thank you, God, for being a promise keeper and never giving up on me even though I chose to go the wrong way. Help me God to trust in you and believe that nothing and no one can keep me like you do. I ask in Jesus' name, Amen

Result of intake:

www.ingramcontent.com/pod-product-compliance
Lightning Source LLC
Chambersburg PA
CBHW071032080526
44587CB00015B/2583